A Metaphorical God

Other Books by Gail Ramshaw

Words around the Fire

Words around the Font

Words around the Table

Words That Sing

For Children:

Sunday Morning

A Metaphorical God

An Abecedary of Images for God

by

Gail Ramshaw

Art by Rita Corbin

LTP

Liturgy Training Publications

Acknowledgments

A Metaphorical God: An Abecedary of Images for God is a revision of *Letters for God's Name*, published in 1984 by Seabury Press, Minneapolis. It was designed by Judy Sweetwood and set in Palatino type by Jim Mellody-Pizzato. Deborah Bogaert was the production editor. Elizabeth Hoffman and Lorraine Schmidt provided additional assistance to the editor, David Philippart. Printed by Commercial Communications, Inc., Waukesha, Wisconsin.

Psalm quotations are taken from *Psalter For the Christian People*, published by The Liturgical Press, Collegeville, Minnesota. Used with permission.

Library of Congress Cataloging-in-Publication Data
Ramshaw, Gail, 1947–

A metaphorical God: an abecedary of images for God /
by Gail Ramshaw; art by Rita Corbin.

p. cm.
Rev ed. of : Letters for God's name. © 1984.
ISBN 1-56854-071-X (paperback)
ISBN 1-56854-128-7 (casebound)
1. Meditations. 2. God—Name—Meditations. 3. Bible.
O.T. Psalms—Meditations. I. Corbin, Rita. II. Ramshaw, Gail,
1947–Letters for God's name. III. Title.
BV4832.2.R245 1995
242—dc20

95-812
CIP

Introduction

On the vaulting elm tree of Christian worship are two major branches. On one are the rituals of corporate worship, their historic forms and approved texts passed down from baptism to baptism. To be Christian is to say these words. On the other branch are the myriad varieties of private devotion, their spontaneity becoming both their glory and their liability. The hope is that private devotion renews our reception of liturgical texts, while the liturgy offers our imaginative explorations their specifically Christian focus. Whether we are sitting on a porch by the lake, traveling on the train to work or discussing the faith with others in the church parlor, our prayer connects us to Sunday morning.

This collection of meditations on the name of God means to be such occasional prayer, short reflections that grow out of and feed back into the communal liturgy of the church. These reflections are based on the psalms, gifts from our Jewish ancestors in the faith. The words of the psalms, born in private prayer, have become standard liturgical texts in our churches. From the Jewish tradition we borrow also a fascination with the alphabet. According to one legend, the first thing God created was the Hebrew alphabet, from which God proceeded to form everything else. In this book we walk through our alphabet to see, if not everything, at least 26 things in God. For while our liturgical texts teach us approved names and metaphors for God, there is always more to God than the liturgy can say.

Suggesting 26 metaphors for God recalls the comments of the seventeenth century Christian poet and priest John Donne. In "Devotions upon Emergent Occasions" he wrote:

> *My God, my God, thou art a direct God, that wouldst be understood literally and according to the plain sense of all that thou sayest. But thou art also a figurative, a metaphorical God, too: a God in whose words there is such a height of figures, such voyages, such peregrinations to fetch remote and precious metaphors, such extensions, such*

spreadings, such curtains of allegories, such third heavens
of hyperboles, so harmonious elocutions . . . ; thou art
the dove that flies.

May the dove of the Spirit of Christ hover nearby as with this primer of
praise we reflect on some facets of our metaphorical God. May we smile back
at Mary and Elizabeth to let them know that they were only beginning the
Christian song.

Feast of the Visitation
1994

NOT EVERY WOMAN was born to bear. Some die still girls, and others molder into the grave having borne fruit other than children ripe or rotten. Such perhaps was Anna, old woman in Advent, eighty-four or more, bearing only a word for all who would hear. Grande dame or hag, this prophet, we do not know. Regal robes or decrepit rags; long white hair, thin and bound in back, or balded by a strange disease which made the children laugh and cringe—we do not know. An early Anselm, a Sophia seeking understanding, or dimwitted and dotty—we cannot guess. But probably this wise widow, seeing visions, praising God, proclaiming truth, snagging the youth with her raspy ecstasy, probably she had borne no children, or none alive, or none at least to claim her. The temple took her—mother superior, sibyl, or bag lady—and she bore a word of God.

Advent is not only maiden Mary, youth and fecundity and hope. One hears from bolder preachers these days, "Advent is like being pregnant"; God is like bearing healthy children; the word of God is a bouncing boy, as if our meeting God were imaged only by a precisely nine-month wait, a day of pain, and then the shared joy of a healthy infant.

Advent, the coming of God, is also Anna, mysterious prophet of the Temple. Meeting God is like a barren old woman with empty breasts and useless womb who waits not a year to bear a child, but for years unknown, and finally waits for death, to catch sight of someone else's baby and to see in that other life the life of God. Meeting God is like the patient doddering dame, trusting until death that God has indeed come into the world. God's advent is heralded abroad by the shaky songs of old woman Anna, sharing a cane with old man Simeon, leaning on each other in the hallways of the courts of God.

It is blasphemous, some say, to see almighty God in Advent's womb. But an antidote to the poison of our simplistic Christmas crêches is to see God in Advent's Anna, the old woman waiting: Anna, offering the Messiah, singing of Alpha, fumbling through a rickety dance, infirm joints cracking to the glory of the Coming One.

Before the mountains were brought forth,
or the land and the earth were born,

   from age to age you are God.
The span of our life is seventy years,
perhaps in strength even eighty;

   yet the sum of them is but labor and sorrow,
   for they pass away quickly and we are gone.
Return, O LIVING ONE; how long will you tarry?

   be gracious to your servants.
Satisfy us by your loving-kindness in the morning;
   so shall we rejoice and be glad all the days of our life.

                              —Psalm 90

MANY OF US are bathed into God as babies.

God as the Bath: the primeval waters holding all earthly life before creation took form; the womb waters protecting and nurturing the preborn child; the dew with its nascent oxygen, cleaning dirty feet; soothing steam for aching limbs; a cold compress for fevered foreheads; tears to wash dust from the eyes.

(But what is this? Romantic Emerson, God-is-water and water-is-God? God as a swashing lakeside, God as the salty sea, God as a mountain spring, God as a tub filled with water and kids on Saturday night?)

All I recall from college biology is looking through a microscope at pond water—a supposedly stagnant pool bathing innumerable forms of life. So Mark Twain wrote a children's adventure of the River bringing freedom to Huck Finn. Yet Twain set the manuscript aside for some years. When he resumed his writing, the northbound turn up the Ohio had been missed during the fog, and the River carried Jim toward ever-crueler slavery. Water, for something so common, is a complicated thing, say those who after the flood's devastation rebuild their shacks on the same river bank. For the water is both their destruction and their lifeline.

The people of God remember many divine baths. Naaman washes in the Jordan and is healed of leprosy. The blind man washes in Siloam's pool and receives his sight. But as the illustrator Peter Spier showed us, what about all the animals who were shut outside, watching Noah's ark as the water rose up their legs? The sea destroys the Egyptian army, and that sea, Leviathan's abode, is ready to drown Jonah. If God is the Bath, is God also the Flood, the waters from which we retreat and the waters within which we flounder?

> *By day and night I cry to you;*
> *all your great waves overwhelm me.*
> —*Psalm 88*

"If I do not wash you, you have no part in me," says Jesus, from whose wounds poured blood and water. "The Mystic Bath," by the seventeenth-century artist Jean Bellegambe, depicts Christ high in the air on the cross, flanked by angels, blood streaming from his wounds. At the foot of Christ is a golden tub, a great baptismal font, filled with naked dancing people. Several more men are climbing into the pool and a woman, beginning to undress, is unfastening her hair. However, this mystic bath of God, this medieval hot tub, is brimming with blood, the naked Christians washing one another with the blood that pours down from the cross.

God as the Bath? God is both the waters of the womb and the frightening flood. Our talk of baptism as the bath which drowns is a way to image God, who is the Bath beyond our knowledge of bathing—a Flood into life, a Washing in blood: not merely a sweet shower on an August afternoon, but the Deluge without which we shrivel up and die. Daily we bathe in this God. We immerse ourselves in the sea of God, overwhelmed by the divine waves, buoyed up again by the undercurrents of God's mercy.

O God, you are my God; eagerly I seek you;
my soul thirsts for you, my flesh faints for you,
as in a barren and dry land where there is no water.
—Psalm 63

AT THE SEDER four cups of wine are raised. The first one sanctifies the feast; the second accompanies the telling of the tale—its volume of wine lessened by ten drops, given up in sorrow for the sufferings of the Egyptians. The third cup, "the cup of blessing," praises God for the meal and for salvation; and the last cup, to anticipate the end time, cries out, "Next year in Jerusalem!" Historians of liturgy like to see a connection between the Jewish cup of blessing and the Christian cup of eucharist, for at table with the disciples Jesus raised the cup after dinner to bless God for salvation.

But there is yet a fifth cup, the cup of Elijah. It stands filled with wine at a place set for that great harbinger of God, because maybe, just maybe, this year, this Passover, God will come here, to our dinner table, in the divine messenger Elijah. At one point during the Seder ritual the door of the house is opened and the outside steps are searched: Was that sound we heard possibly Elijah's knock? No, I can't see Elijah there after all. But sometime during the evening, perhaps as the children are searching for the hidden matzo, the cup gets mysteriously drained, and the children return to table to wonder whether God did, after all, send Elijah that year.

There is a way that we can see Elijah's cup as the one we Christians drain at the eucharistic meal. We can imagine that this holy cup is the one waiting through the ages to delight God's messenger, the draught which heralds the new age. Each eucharist is a celebration of the resurrection, each resurrection a Passover: This cup is reserved for and finally drunk by the one sent by God. It is as if we were sharing a meal of hope, and we opened the door because we thought we heard a knock; or perhaps the doors were locked for fear, and suddenly God has sent One to be at table with us. By this new Elijah the meal is sanctified as never before. God is present, and the meal has been transformed into a time of wonder. We add our experiences to the tales of long ago, and we tell the stories again: Sarah prepared dinner for God at Mamre; God ate and drank with Moses and the elders; we knew him at the breaking of bread; Elijah's cup is drained, at this meal, by God.

"Are you able to drink the cup that I drink?" asks Jesus of his faithful ones. For there is also the cup of wrath:

> *For in the hand of the LIVING GOD there is a cup,*
> *full of spiced and foaming wine—the LIVING ONE pours*
> *it out—*
> *and all the wicked of the earth shall drink and drain the dregs.*
> *—Psalm 75*

Enraged Jeremiah demands that the world's evil ones be given the poisonous cup. Yet a stained-glass window in a Paris church depicts the winepress of God; intended to squeeze out the wine from the earth's sour grapes, it is instead pressing down on Christ, and his blood seeps out from his veins into the waiting chalices. And in the waiting room of an oncology surgeon in St. Paul, Minnesota, is a depiction of the Last Supper, the cup being filled with the tears of God and the bloody sweat of Jesus. For the drink poured for Jesus is not only the goblet of Elijah but also the vinegar of God's wrath and sorrow. "Abba, remove this cup from me," he begged.

Among the most revered of Christian artifacts have been chalices, those great jeweled golden goblets, the ornate designs and engraved scenes fervently trying to make the outside of the cup worthy of its contents. But the wonder is not the spun silver depiction of Caleb and Joshua lugging back to camp a mammoth bunch of grapes, nor the gems which rivaled the sovereign's crown. The wonder is the wine, drinking the new covenant with God, the holy grail of the life of the one who drained the dregs of suffering. "Drink me," the bottle said to Alice: and so we do, and, with Alice, are transformed. Yet, inexplicably, some omit the cup, or replace it with glass jiggers, as if God were a sip, bottoms-up, a quarter-teaspoon measured out in the prescription of healing me. The four-year-old said, "It's funny: We drink God in the wine." Indeed, the finest, most precious article of our worship ought to be the cup, this container of God, which in pouring Christ into us all pours us into one another and so into God.

O God, you are my portion and my cup;
  in your presence there is fullness of joy,
  and in your right hand are pleasures for evermore.
                    —Psalm 16

DAVID WAS FIRST a shepherd who roamed the wilds, living in a tent and caring for animals. The rugged life of compassion, the brute strength of the herdsman, making a living by protecting dirty, stupid sheep: This was David, the shepherd. David was later a warrior with slingshots and arrows, swords and chariots. Vanquishing the enemy, creating a homeland—this was David, the warrior. David was last a king, the authority of the civilized city, the protector of the gates, the judge for the oppressed, commanding homage. From the chaos of warring towns, he molded a nation: David, the king. David was always a singer, fingering beauty on his harp, shaping praise into a psalm, offering songs for the sheep, for the throne and for the people. David the singer plucked the harp to pacify the mad Saul and to acclaim the greatness of God.

Thus was David the epitome of God's ancient people, the chief of the chosen ones, and a sign of the promise. And in a kind of linguistic square dance in which partners get interchanged, it is not only that David is the model Jew because, acclaimed by God, he is shepherd and king and singer, but also that the LIVING GOD, acclaimed by David and all the people, is shepherd, warrior, king and singer.

God is shepherd, leading the flock of Israel, tending the ewes, saving the strays, finding pasture, watering the infirm, bringing them home:

> *My shepherd is the LIVING GOD;*
> *I shall not be in want.*
> *You make me lie down in green pastures*
> *and lead me beside still waters.*
>
> *— Psalm 23*

God is warrior, attacking the enemy, destroying evil. Our Robin Hood, slaying Goliaths with small smooth stones:

> *God trains my hands for battle*
> *and my arms for bending even a bow of bronze.*

> *You have given me your shield of victory;*
> *you have put my enemies to flight.*
>
> —*Psalm 18*

God is the sovereign, protecting the city, ruling over the people, establishing justice, heeding the poor, sitting on that throne before which we subject ourselves in awe:

> *O mighty sovereign, lover of justice,*
> *you have established equity;*
> *you have executed justice*
> *and righteousness in Jacob.*
>
> —*Psalm 99*

God is singer, maker of beauty, weaver of harmony, whose melody is grace, whose rhythm is justice. Better yet, God is the song, the only music worth singing, the *cantus firmus* of the universe, the obbligato of salvation:

> *Give thanks to the LIVING ONE, who is good,*
> *whose mercy endures forever.*
> *The LIVING ONE is my strength and my song,*
> *and has become my salvation.*
>
> —*Psalm 118*

But we ask: In which direction do the metaphors flow? Is David acclaimed because he is made in the likeness of God, or is God described in recognizable ways because we already honor David? Who is the God beyond the shepherd, the warrior, the king, the song? Who is the God beyond the metaphors upon which our minds rely? Had there been no David, what would be divine?

We are given D, only to search beyond it.

EXSULTET JAM ANGELICA turba caelorum;
exsultent divina mysteria. . . .

With these words ringing from ancient times down to the present, the deacon proclaims Easter. In most translations in contemporary English, the deacon's poem begins, "Rejoice!" but still the chant is called the Exsultet, the Leaping Up for Joy, a jumping up from the grave in delight.

The poem has its setting: a dark nave, a crowd in the night keeping vigil, a white-robed deacon bearing high a large lit candle. The enormous size of some medieval paschal candlestands makes us wonder whether the candle would not have been too heavy to be borne. But even nowadays the candle glows high above our heads, a phallic light over the womb waters in the fecund night. Around this single flame gathers the congregation, and the Exsultet is chanted. The angel choirs, the earth and "its ancient darkness," the church, and the congregation are to exult, to leap for joy, at the brilliant splendor, the radiant brightness, of the single candle.

("This one candle?!"

"Well, no, Christ."

"Well, why not sing to Christ, instead of to the candle?"

"Well, because! Besides, it's not to the candle.")

The single candle is an icon before us, becoming other than it is, receiving us other than we are, as the chant transforms words to other than they appear. We proclaim the Exsultet, we leap up for joy because, on this Saturday night, the debt of Adam is repaid; the lamb's blood is smeared on our door; Israel crosses the sea; sinners are restored to holiness; the chains of death are snapped; hell is harrowed; and earth is wed to heaven. The tragedy of Eden is "a happy fault." The morning star, the resurrected Jesus and this single burning candle are superimposed, intermingled; and where our recently purchased paschal candle stops and where Christ takes over, the poem will not say. So it is that the deacon, with eyes straining in the darkened church to make out the words of the chant, exults over the spectacular brilliance of the room!

You, O LIVING ONE, are my lamp;
my God, you make my darkness bright.
—Psalm 18

Easter celebrations in the daytime are blind to this part of God's name, the shining of light in darkness. On the sunny morning, boasting new clothes, Easter bonnets, white lilies, shiny trumpets, daffodil corsages, we sing easily about seeds growing into bright flowers. But in what is called the dead of night, to exult over one single candle and to acclaim it God's beacon: This calls for faith in the resurrection.

For in the night it is not so much that we exalt God, giving God glory, singing a song of praise. It is rather that we exult in God as we leap up out of the dark and out from the grave, leap up in God. Not only do we leap up because of God, but we leap up in God: We are entombed, but God surrounds our tomb; and so we leap out of death into God. Perhaps, then, God is the darkness of the night into which we leap, as well as the candle around which we exult.

You will shelter them,

so that those who love your name may exult in you.

—Psalm 5

FOR SOME FOLK, life is a feast. Oh, not that their hearts are daily overflowing with happiness, their every desire met; no, such a heaven rarely occurs. But one's life might yet be a feast: three meals a day of a variety of plenteous foods, with cloth napkins and silver napkin rings, a lit candle every suppertime, good china on Sundays, the Waterford bowl full of fruit salad. On special occasions you use the pointy spoons for grapefruit, and you sneak a peek at the elders, just as the old Danish peasants at Babette's feast watched how the worldy-wise soldier ate the quail's head properly. Perhaps such folk imagine God to be a feast. They know of plenty, and for the believer, God is the most plenteous.

But for others life is famine. Entire chaotic countries starve the poor so that the rich can watch television in their limousines. Crops are neglected during wartime, and political upheaval prohibits the food distribution centers from functioning effectively. I have shopped in a cut-rate grocery store near my neighborhood, and the food is cheap and fake—airy bread and soy meat. The store does not stock fresh produce. The children load up on sugar snacks on their way to school, as if Twinkies were food. Surely for some of these people, God must be the famine that is their lives.

The people of the scriptures knew such famine. The Israelites, hungry in the desert, long for the onions and garlic of Egypt. The widow of Zeraphath is preparing her very last meal. Some see famine as an avenging God who sends not rain but divine judgment upon sinners. Or famine is a test of faith, as if our cruel God measured human trust in times of agony on a ten-point scale, nine points for that woman praising as she starves.

"You have fed them with the bread of tears; you have given them bowls of tears to drink" (Psalm 80), writes a psalmist, begging for divine mercy on a suffering people, pleading with a God whose middle name is Famine.

But Jews and Christians read in the scriptures the hope of a feast in the future. Food and wine aplenty will be served up free of charge to all peoples on the mountain of God; there will be feasting forever in God's time of joy. In the book of Revelation, the feast is a primary image of future life with God, divinity enjoyed after death, a heavenly state beyond earthly needs. In the religious ecstasy of just such a vision the psalmist says:

> *They feast upon the abundance of your house;*
> *you give them drink from the river of your delights.*
> —*Psalm 36*

But religion is not that simplistic, feast or famine, famine or feast. For some people who feast daily, God is an empty shelf. For some who starve, God fills them with song, if not food. Perhaps we are being adolescent, reveling in the extremes: Perhaps God is beyond feast or famine. Perhaps God is food, the plain and simple sustenance of life. Such a God would give enough manna, but not enough to hoard. The widow's larder would have enough oil and meal for each day.

Jesus would serve the thousands on the mountainside one serving each of a poor child's lunch of bread and fish.

God as food is enough: not the gorgeous body nor the famished flesh, but the bones beneath; neither the spring flowers nor the tumbleweed, but the soil under them both. To the whole created order God is food, lifeblood, breath;

> *You make grass grow for flocks and herds*
> *and plants to serve humankind;*
> *the lions roar after their prey*
> *and seek their food from God.*
> *all of them look to you*
> *to give them food in due season.*
>
> *—Psalm 104*

Such a God is for the wolves and the deer, for the spiders and the humans: not spectacularly abundant for some, a dazzling display of divine power for the religious few, nor the agony of emptiness, pitiful privation for the many. God as food is there, the ground of all being, mother earth maintaining the universe. Such a God might serve a piece of bread and a swallow of wine, and would know that it is enough.

But here's the question: If God were food, neither famine nor feast, could we be content?

GOD'S GAZE IS good, we like to say. For our language assumes that God has eyes, that God sees everything, that God gazes on the faithful. We would hardly draw God as a great nose or a mammoth mouth, but even our God is pictured sometimes as a single open eye in the center of a triangle. That eye of course would never blink, and even when tears would wash it of the world's dust, it would gaze through the tears with penetrating mercy. Copying the native Huichols of central Mexico, we have taught our children to make "gods' eyes" at summer camp, and whether of Popsicle sticks and yellow yarn or of crafted woods and fine woven threads, the sign is the same: The four corners of the earth cross, marking the place of the gaze of God. And so we like to pray:

> O LIVING ONE, you look down from heaven,
>   and behold all the people in the world.
> From where you sit enthroned you turn your gaze
>   on all who dwell on the earth.

Behold, your eye, O LIVING ONE, is upon those who fear you,
on those who wait upon your love.

—Psalm 33

I will gaze on you, says God, says the lover to the beloved. My look will not waver; on you I am fixed. And so we have the made-up word "gazebo," as if we were speaking Latin to say "I will gaze," and we build a white canopy in the garden where lovers can gaze at each other and together gaze at the sea. Indeed, the liturgy is one such stupendous gazebo, intricate, glistening, within which God gazes at us and we together gaze at God.

But (yes, there is always a but) the gaze of God is not only the beloved one making eyes at her sweetheart. The testimony of the Hebrew people is that a human being cannot endure the prolonged gaze of God. Moses can glimpse only on God's backside, for even the highest human holiness cannot meet the divine eyes. We hide with Adam and Eve in the bushes of Eden. We cower with the tax collector behind the pillar. We run with Peter from the courtyard. So although sometimes we yearn for God's gaze, sometimes we sing a different psalm:

> *Take your affliction from me;*
> *I am worn down by the blows of your hand.*
> *Turn your gaze from me, that I may be glad again,*
> *before I go my way and am no more.*
>
> *—Psalm 39*

G: What is G? God's gaze, searing us through, penetrating us, with joy or despair, differently on different days.

IT WAS MARCH 1, a routine day at the gynecologist's office. By the door there sat a forty-some-year-old Irish Catholic woman, worn, white with the white of illness added to the white of Irish, nine months pregnant with her fifth child: "I've three boys and a girl; we'll call the baby Brian." Even while sitting still, she panted for breath and waved a copy of *People* magazine to cool herself. She had always been constipated during her pregnancies, but this was terrible, this was five days. . . . In a corner sat an old white woman, short gray hair, breathing unevenly; she had been led into the waiting room by a black attendant. So old! How could something still be wrong with her womb? How long has it been since she was a well woman? In another corner was a middle-aged woman, dressed in a gray flannel suit, getting a checkup after a miscarriage. She said she felt rather well, no longer convinced that the physicians and the anesthetist had spent that half hour kicking her in the belly. And in the fourth corner was the inevitable high-school girl, designer jeans, blank face, dazed eyes, walled into loneliness, holding her Dixie cup of urine, awaiting word on a test that would prove positive. The receptionist spoke loudly into the phone: a woman with severe pains, another woman bleeding.

Into this room of unhealth bounced a new mother for her two-week checkup, grinning her face apart, her newborn squalling until its mouth was filled with her breast. Apologetic of all this life, the nurses explained: "Babies are always lovely after a Cesarean."

> *Have pity on me, O LIVING GOD, for I am weak;*
> *heal me, O LIVING ONE, for my bones are racked.*
> *—Psalm 6*

All this unhealth, and it was March 1, the day George Herbert had died 350 years before:

> *My flesh began unto my soul in pain,*
> *Sicknesses cleave my bones;*

Consuming agues dwell in ev'ry vein;
  And tune my breath to grones.
Sorrow was all my soul; I scarce beleeved,
Till grief did tell me roundly, that I lived.

All those women and George Herbert pleading for health, for bodies that work: Closer than Calcutta is sorrow to the marrow. We plead for the day when the scar is healed and we feel its fierce line no more. We plead for a healthy child, a healthy mother.

And so we plead for God, God our health, God who sometimes gives health, but not always—no, not even to those who pray most piously—some health to some people, as if health were each single time a miracle, a gift of God's self made on this special occasion to a people more acquainted with pain.

Or more: to plead for God as if we really trusted that God is Health, that being in God is being in health, little and big death notwithstanding.

Let your ways be known upon earth,
  your saving health among all nations.
Let the peoples praise you, O God;
  let all the peoples praise you.

—Psalm 67

BECAUSE OF THE incarnation there are icons, say Orthodox Christians.

Of course we cannot draw a picture of God! Nonsense, to think we can depict divinity! Yet since God became human, it is almost as if God wants to be seen, choosing a form which can be drawn, approving the desire of our curious eyes. This God of the incarnation, say Orthodox Christians, is imaged in the icon. The iconographer paints Christ, Mary and the saints, their humanity elongated beyond nature, their sanctified eyes drawing us into the depths of their redeemed souls, the depiction a way of glimpsing the incarnate God, the infinity beyond. The image expresses humankind on its way to becoming divine by imaging Christ, who was divinity in the flesh. So, say these Christians, we see into God through the icon.

And we who are weary of picture after picture of sexy Eve and a female-headed serpent undertaking to effect the human fall delight at the icon of Christ's descent into hell. Christ has trampled down the door of Hades and with arms outstretched is pulling Eve and Adam up from death to life. Christ's merciful arms are the icon of divinity, and Eve, gracefully robed, the icon not of the damned but of the saved.

"To represent the God of Sabaoth (that is, the Father) on icons with a gray beard, with his only Son on his lap, and a dove between them, is exceedingly absurd and unseemly," spoke the Great Moscow Council in 1667. How icons pictured God was to recall the Genesis story of God's first appearance to the faithful, when God came for dinner to the tent of Abraham and Sarah. God comes, God speaks, but isn't it three persons we see? Yet the narrative calls them angels! How is it that we cannot know with whom we speak? Who is this who so mysteriously escapes our categories? Early icons showed Abraham and Sarah serving their guests a tableful of food, but Andrei Rublev purified the icon, depicting the Trinity as three winged guests, three glimmerings of divine power through whom God chose to be seen.

This God we worship—looking for Eve, dining with Sarah and Abraham, showing Moses the divine backside, born in Jesus, alive in the saints, proclaiming in the icon—this God must want to be seen.

The Hebrews were right: We do not sculpt God. But Christ, the icon of God, has shared a meal with us, and in the faces of all Christ's body, we see God.

> *Deliver me, O LIVING ONE, by your hand*
>   *from those whose portion in life is this world.*
> *At my vindication I shall see your face;*
>   *when I awake, I shall be satisfied, beholding your likeness.*
>   *—Psalm 17*

LEVITICUS SAYS THAT on Mount Sinai God instructed Moses in the way of the Jubilee. Every seven years the land would have a sabbatical: no crops planted, not even straggling shoots harvested. It was a year to rest in God. But once every 50 years would come the Jubilee itself, and in that year the land lying fallow would be the least of the signs of the time of rest. The trumpet would blow, and families would reassemble. Land sold to pay off loans would be given back. Houses that the rich had acquired from the poor would be returned. People indentured to settle great debts would be released. It was a free redemption, all the way around, debts paid off because they were completely forgiven.

So here we have a man; perhaps he is named Joshua. Middle-aged, bonded as a child to pay off his family debt, he works the quarries to hack out stone or guards the city gates through the night. His only thought: the Jubilee is coming. Will that year really come? Will all the people recognize it, acclaim it, live out its spirit? Joshua keeps hoping. He waits each night for the morning star. He hopes for forgiveness of all debts; he hopes to arise from the pit; he hopes for a new morning to shine; he hopes for the mercy of freedom.

Daily he prays:

> *Out of the depths have I called to you, O LIVING GOD;*
> *O LIVING ONE, hear my voice;*
> *let your ears consider well the voice of my supplication.*
> *I wait for you, O LIVING ONE; my soul is waiting;*
> *in the LIVING GOD'S word is my hope.*
> *My soul waits for the LIVING ONE,*
> *more than sentries for the morning,*
> *more than sentries for the morning.*
>
> – *Psalm 130*

He knows that in praying for the Jubilee he is hoping for God. For when the Jubilee did roll around, it would be as if God were visiting the land, a guest of the nation, inhabiting the very soil, making all things free and new, reinstating the Garden of Eden.

But what if the Jubilee eludes the calendar, if the banks accidentally forget that next year the debtors are exonerated, if repeated crops ruin the soil, if the poor are always with us? What if we, searching the scriptures, ascertain the date of the rapture, and once again God stands us up? Perhaps, like God, the Jubilee was only a fairy tale fashioned by reactionaries befuddled by urban reality. How can we know?

We cannot know. We wait. We trust that the Jubilee will come: Joshua will reclaim the family farm; Ruth, now destitute, will become great-grandmother of a king; all the faithful will rise from the dead. Daily we pray: O God, send your Jubilee. And if you will not come in metaphor, then come as your very self.

K . . . K. WHAT DOES K say about God? Key, king, koinonia . . . until there in the unabridged dictionary was "K, kuphar, a small round boat of willow covered with skins used on the Euphrates." Well.

> *By the waters of Babylon we sat down and wept,*
> *when we remembered you, O Zion.*
>
> *—Psalm 137*

Twenty-five hundred years ago they were there, Jews exiled in Babylon, weeping into the river Euphrates. They could not drown their songs in the Euphrates—the river is too shallow—but their joys were flooded away. Singing the psalms in a strange land, how they would have wished for such a small round boat—a kuphar —to carry them safely up the river and back to the Holy Land. God already had provided the willows lining the Euphrates. Perhaps God would provide also the animal skins: Hadn't Adam and Eve received their needed skins from God? One can hear the faithful, choking on Zion's songs, groaning, ah! for a kuphar, a kuphar to take us home.

Like the Ganges, the cries flow on. Henry Muhlenberg, on board ship for weeks traveling from Germany to colonial America to begin life as a Lutheran missionary, recorded the anguish of the passengers, their agonizing thirst, the thirst of even the rats who licked the sweat off his face as he slept. And the boat people, who thought they were headed to freedom, find themselves sailing only into storm, starvation and border police. Ah, for a kuphar, for our kuphar!

It is still the same. Along with our praises rises the plea that a boat will come our way, taking us from slavery back to our own free land. We beg for a ship to save us from the stormy wind by sailing us back to safety. We hope to join Reepicheep in his coracle gliding through the lilied sea straight into Aslan's country.

Then were they glad because of the calm;
    and God brought them to the harbor they were bound for.
                                        —Psalm 107

One boat has been granted, one kuphar for our Euphrates, one ark for our flood. We sit each week on its wooden benches, in that nave of ours, and sail home to God, in God. For the kuphar God sends is the kuphar God is.

WATCHING MY FRIENDS and relatives raise their children, I came to see the playpen, or its absence, as an early indicator of the family's dearest values. Some relied on a playpen filled with toys and picture books to provide the entire family an hour of freedom, but others wouldn't have dreamt of owning such a barbarous torture chamber. So it has come to be that while some families mark clear boundaries, with closed doors, family meals at 6:00 PM and cloth napkins laundered weekly, in other homes a spontaneous, carefree chaos prevails.

The psalmists are the pro-playpen sort. The Hebrew poets who drafted the praises of God's law knew nothing of individual freedom. Only in community could the family gather at Seder, the ten men assemble at prayer, the midwives assist at birth. And when we wake in the morning in a crowded family, how do we know how to live? The psalmists agree: Thanks be to God for the law. We do not always see God near our table, at our tasks, by our bed, but the mark of God is in the law. By living the law we live with God, and that, according to the psalmists, is the highest human goal.

The law shines as God's light among us,

> *more to be desired than gold,*
> *more than much fine gold,*
> *sweeter far than honey,*
> *than honey in the comb.*

—Psalm 19

In the 176 verses of psalm 119, the praise of God's glistening law—that is, God's decrees, commandments, statutes, word, judgments, precepts, ordinances, promise, way—is arranged in alphabetical stanzas, for the poet believed that from God's law originates all wholesome human communication. In medieval art we see depictions of Pentecost, with the tongues of fire on the apostles' heads, paralleled with pictures of Moses presenting the tablets of the law to the Israelites.

God comes in the flames of the Spirit no more than in the letters of the law.

But for Christians, "law" cannot mean the 613 commands of the Torah. Even the ten commandments need some adjustment, adapting "the Sabbath day" to mean Sunday so that the law can be honored among us. For Christians, "God-with-us," the presence of God by which we live, the divine way dispensing shalom into our community, the law for us, is Christ. Awakening in the morning in a crowded family, how do we know how to live? With the Spirit of Christ within, our way is lighted, our family meals sweet. Each other is Christ, and if we look with intent to love, we see flames flickering on the crown of everyone's head.

The law of Christ (an oxymoron worth our meditation) makes our world not as small as a playpen but as boundless as the universe. Perhaps one thing "heaven" means is that the universe itself will have to expand when Christ resides in all its corners. Living with this law we are not cramped into a cage but are dancing together in a ballroom whose walls are pushing out the edge of the solar system; and God is with us, teaching us the steps.

ONCE UPON A time there was a young girl living in a land of terror. The wicked king had decreed the murder of the boy babies of the aliens. Now the young girl had a baby brother, newly born, still weeping quietly, held constantly at his mother's breast so that his crying was quickly stilled. But the day that his cry became too loud, his mother decided to hide the child. She made a basket of rushes, painted it watertight, and floated it in the river, hiding it in the rushes alongside the shore. The girl had the task of watching. She was to babysit, to guard the helpless boy, to embrace the child with her eyes, at least. And the girl did well: Her brother Moses was saved. She protected him from evil, she devised a rescue, she brought him home again to warmth and milk and life. The young girl's name was Miriam.

Much later there was a woman of God who bore three children. Without much assistance from her husband, she strove to raise her children in a life of grace. But she was plagued especially by her eldest and wayward son. She prayed for that son, disciplined him, and followed him when he ran away. She offered him love, always more love, wept over his foolishness, and invited him to God. And the woman did well: Her son Augustine was saved. She had taught him to love; she had forgiven him. She had persevered beyond all expectation and brought him home to the church, to baptism and to life. The woman's name was Monica.

> *You are the LIVING ONE;*
> *do not withhold your compassion from me;*
> > *let your love and your faithfulness keep me safe for ever.*
> *For innumerable troubles have crowded upon me;*
> *my sins have overtaken me, and I cannot see;*
> > *they are more in number than the hairs of my head,*
> > *and my heart fails me.*
> *Be pleased, O LIVING GOD, to deliver me;*
> > *O LIVING ONE, make haste to help me.*

You are my helper and my deliverer;
do not tarry, O my God.

—Psalm 40

And also we, helpless infants who must be kept safe, runaway children chased by our sins, we need a basket to protect us, a great round font in which to wash ourselves free. Also we rise up from the water to join Moses in Miriam's song: "I will sing to you, for you triumphed gloriously." And Monica smiles as Augustine adds his stanza, in Latin, of course, *"Te Deum laudamus."*

Miriam; Monica. A girl who saved her brother; a woman who loved her son. Moses is freed from innumerable troubles; sin did not overtake Augustine. Miriam, Monica: In case you have not guessed, two of the countless names for God.

THOSE CURIOUS CELIBATE Christian communities we call the Shakers forbade ornamentation of every kind: no fancy dress, no decorations, no jewelry, no art. Perfectly plain design, uncluttered by unnecessary additions, constituted beauty for them. But in the 1850s, some Shaker women began to have visions, and since the visions came from their founder Ann Lee or from the divine Holy Mother Wisdom herself, the women were allowed to record their visions in "spirit-drawings." You can see these drawings in museums now, and reproductions of them in histories of the Shakers: charming, precise, primitive; geometric designs, heart-shaped leaves, fanciful flowers, bizarre birds, all labeled with the strangest of phrases. One spirit-drawing depicts "the choicest of treasures" from Mother Wisdom, "a cage of singing birds from Sarah of old," "a dove of peace," "a trumpet from Moses, to reveal the word of God to the nations." My favorite is a tiny chain, blue links with gold, labeled "a necklace from the Woman of Samaria."

N, necklace. To that community in which both necklaces and husbands were taboo came a promise of a divine treasure to come, worn not now, oh no, but presented someday by divine Wisdom herself: a necklace from the Samaritan floozy-turned-catechumen. Is it that when she of the five-and-a-half husbands entered God's eternity, she wore a knock-out necklace, one jewel for each marriage promise, one gold link for each attempt at love? Is it that in heaven she needs her jewelry no longer, and so, in one of God's surprises, the Shaker visionary stands to inherit? Or is it that God, seeing the Samaritan woman coming from far off, ran to her, embraced and kissed her, and presented her with gorgeous clothes and a spectacular necklace?

We now stand ill-dressed in good company: Eve and Adam, awaiting garments of animal skins; the people of Israel, their outfits 40 years old; the wedding guest, caught wearing jeans; the catechumens, stripped down and shivering. Some wear shrouds, and there is the soldier with a seamless tunic, won while on duty at Calvary. But for the marriage of the Lamb, we must adorn ourselves with jewels; we must don our crowns; we must fasten our necklaces.

What might that necklace be like? Hildegard of Bingen saw a pearl choker tight around the neck of the ancient serpent, each pearl a song of praise, "strung upon the word of God." With the serpent finally dead and gone, perhaps the pearls will be mine. Gertrude the Great imagined she already wore a brilliant necklace, made from Christ's shining wounds: Some jewelry, Gertrude! But imagine the necklace God might give: a diamond of God's tears, a ruby of God's blood, an emerald from the tree of life, and endless gold links of divine mercy. The necklace would be what God is: a circle of radiant grace.

> *You have turned my wailing into dancing:*
> *you have put off my sack-cloth and clothed me with joy.*
> *Therefore my heart sings to you without ceasing;*
> *O LIVING ONE, my God, I will give you thanks for ever.*
> *—Psalm 30*

THE OBOE'S SOUND resists description. The words we use—nasal, twangy—connote unpleasantness. But the expert oboist (and if you have heard only the oboe in the high school band, you have not heard what I have heard), the consummate oboist, one of the world's best, creating that extraordinary tone, perhaps laying a high G# pianissimo on the very edge of your hearing—that sound is not nasal. That oboe—odd, penetrating—leaves the air altered. Stunned, one keeps vigil for the approaching sound by not breathing. Standards for sound have now changed. All hearing is now in relationship to that oboe solo.

But let's stop talking about it. Talk about music, like talk about God, is too easily vague babble. Words should say only, "Listen to that oboe."

One September evening I heard the principal oboist of the New York Philharmonic perform a solo passage in a contemporary composition. And I said, "There is more about God in that oboe than in most sermons I've heard." But lest you think me only another one of those church musicians who prattle on as if the liturgy is best thought of as a sacred concert and singing a cantata better than proclaiming the readings, let me explain.

It was not that there was gospel in that oboe. Christ was not proclaimed, and incarnation is not about musical instruments. But the oboe sounded out against shallow biblical interpretations and scrimpy piety, sermons in which the vision of God is limited and our vision, then, further obscured. At least with the oboe the universe had to expand in order to contain the sound. Perception itself had trembled. Words had stopped. The oboe had suggested the absolute. And so, unlike trivial sermons, the oboe had pointed toward God.

Being pointed toward God is not everything; it alone cannot save. But it is at least something. It is something worth the tremble.

The voice of the LIVING ONE is a powerful voice;
the voice of the LIVING ONE is a voice of splendor.
The voice of the LIVING ONE breaks the cedar trees;

the LIVING ONE breaks the cedars of Lebanon.
The voice of the LIVING ONE makes the oak trees writhe
and strips the forests bare.
And in the temple of the LIVING GOD
all are crying, "Glory!"

—Psalm 29

"THE PINIONS OF God will protect you."

P is for peacock, the paradise bird of stunning beauty, whose tail has 100 eyes and whose flesh, it is said, does not decay. And so God is a peacock, immortality and glory and iridescent dress.

P is for pelican. The story says that in a rage the father pelican murdered his young and that the mother pelican revived her children by sprinkling on them the blood she let from her own breast. In his hymn "Adoro Te Devoto," Thomas Aquinas recalls the myth by calling Jesus "pie pellicane." (But Cardinal Newman edited that out, leaving Jesus only as the pure font.) And so God is a pelican, feeding her children with her own blood.

P is for phoenix. After living 1000 years in the grove of Paradise, the phoenix flies to earth, builds a death-nest of the finest spices and sets itself on fire. From the ashes, three days later, emerges the new young phoenix; for there is only one phoenix alive at any one time. Its plumage is brilliant scarlet and gold. And so God is a phoenix, the only one, which offers itself for self-immolation and three days later is revived for life.

God's pinions: a nimbus shimmering blue-green; a bloody white breast; scarlet, then ash, then gold. A God with feathers? Divine plumes? Yet we sing, "Lord Jesus, since you love me, now spread your wings above me," and God describes the escape from Egypt as a flight on eagle's wings. That eagle flies through the psalms, the mother eagle pushing her young out of the nest to teach them to fly, but swooping down underneath to catch them with her wings in case they fall. And if not a soaring eagle, then a descending dove: For the divine Spirit hovered over the head of Jesus at his baptism, hovering as on creation day, bringing forth unprecedented life.

> *Be merciful to me, O God, be merciful,*
> *for I have taken refuge in you;*
> *in the shadow of your wings will I take refuge*
> *until this time of trouble has gone by.*
> *—Psalm 57*

God's pinions: Perhaps in the end-time authors and poets, still compulsively writing about the divine names, will be graced with a quill pen plucked from the plumage of God.

WHAT IF GOD were Queen of heaven?

If our God were Queen of heaven, we could burn incense to her and bake cakes for her, and our adoration would be acceptable.

If our God were Queen of heaven, her crown would rest on hair long and curly and rainbowed, and we could grab onto that hair as we nursed and so would be saved from falling. Her shining face, smooth and clear as light, would enliven the universe. And when we were poor, the Queen would take from her necklace flowing with pearls and opals and every colored gem perhaps an amber to fill our needs. The resplendent gold of her majestic robe would be what we call the sun, and the sheen of her nightdress the moon. Her rule would reach to the deepest corners of the darkness; her beauty would rout the devils and her wisdom would rear the world. Her royal blood would give us divinity. Our being born again in God would be a nativity from the divine womb, God's labor an agony of necessity; for we know it is the essence of the reign of our Queen to love with mercy. Our death would be, as with all babies, a going home to mother. Our life would be, as with heirs apparent, following in the train of the Queen.

Hebrew poetry and Christian metaphor have made our divine Sovereign only a king. But a king, say the fairy tales, requires a queen. The universe must be balanced. So the court was filled: The Queen is Mary, bearing the king's son and wedded to Christ the King. She was the first to enter God's reign, from the moment of her birth and since the moment of her death accepting God's crown of grace. Like Queen Esther, she takes our petitions to the throne.

And the Queen is the church, which is sometimes a virgin, sometimes a wanton, always the desired, the divine lover, married to God and reigning with God over all of creation. The rabbis too played word games, and God reigned as king with the divine spirit, Ruah, or with law, Torah, or with wisdom, Hokmah, or with the holy space of divine presence, Shekinah—these feminine nouns a kind of queen attending the royal throne.

But it could have been another set of images as well. The Sovereign of heaven and earth is also a womb of mercy, a majesty of grace and beauty, one who creates the royal children out of herself:

> *In the beauty of holiness have I begotten you,*
> *like dew from the womb of the morning.*
> —*Psalm 110*

The people of God could be a symbolic man, perhaps the Mortal One of Daniel's vision, who serves the divine monarch by accompanying her pangs of life-giving. Or the Sovereign could be the Queen and we all be Mary, divine generation, dynasty of Amazons, sharing in the world's labor: the first birth, like creation, a birth unto death; and the rebirth, like the resurrection, a birth unto life.

The majesty of the Sovereign has terrified the world. She has borne us in pain and nursed us with care; and we, like Jewish children, carry her blood and are royal from rebirth in her. For our God is Queen of all the earth, and adoration of her splendor is our life.

> *To you I lift up my eyes,*
>   *to you enthroned in the heavens.*
> *As the eyes of servants look to the hand of their masters,*
>   *and the eyes of a maid to the hand of her mistress,*
> *So our eyes look to the LIVING ONE, our God,*
>   *until you show us your mercy.*
>
> *—Psalm 123*

But it is all so many words, noises grunting out adoration, a cat purring affection, babble ill-informed and misdirected, an alphabet shouted out into the abyss, preceded by a prayer that the angels will shape it into a canticle of praise.

WHEN SUPPERTIME CAME and all my fair-skinned family had soaked up enough sun to make us miserable, we would leave the sandy beach and hike up to the rocky point where picnics could be spread out on boulders. I was young, and I would choose my own private crag, one partway into the salty water so my toes could play with the barnacles, and there I would sup atop a rock in the sea.

It is harder, now, to find rocks so satisfying as were those boulders, personal palisades between the poison ivy and the sea. The search is not mine alone: The stories are filled with an archetypal search for the rock, the rock that is higher than I, the rock on which to build, the rock that makes me secure. Even in the desert the desire for a rock is there: stone against the shifting sands, a shade from the scalding sun. And to the Hebrew's surprise, the rock splits open, and from the great fissure gushes water—both rock and water at once—so that the people might survive. And the rabbis later said that the rock followed the people around the desert for all forty years, their security, their shade, their water supply keeping up with the crowd.

The disciples too needed a rock, and as Paul teaches, using the language of the ancient wilderness travels, "the rock was Christ." And so Christ found, or founded, a rock, and on Peter was built a city, and Rome became a kind of rock as Jerusalem had been, the foundation stone of a people and the navel of the world. Also from this rock flowed water, the water in all those ancient baptistries now dry to tourists' cameras, as water had flowed from his side the hour the Rock was cleft.

> *God alone is my rock and my salvation,*
> *my stronghold, so that I shall not be shaken.*
> *—Psalm 62*

When Moses doubts the graciousness of God and begs to see God's glory, God says, "The face of the glory of my graciousness is more than you can bear: Even to glimpse my backside, you'd best let this rock shield you." We join with Moses singing the psalm in Deuteronomy, praising the Rock whose work is perfect, whose ways are just, who labored to bear us, God's cleft opening up and we emerging to live.

We are born of the Rock that is God; we stand on the Rock that is Christ; we live by the water outpouring; and at our death the rock of our tomb will be the doorway to God.

FOR MANY OF us, the images of warfare have lost their allure. The cry of the patriot, "Better dead than red," sounds like ancient rhetoric, or a misguided value from an earlier time when nations were insular and bombs unknown. In Beowulf's English, the word for "adult male" was the same as the word for "warrior." But speaking 1200 years later, at least I am attracted more by the bishops' appeal for nuclear disarmament than by the medals on a soldier's uniform. They say that World War II was different: My uncle died in that valor which saved the world from a madman and from the vipers flourishing around him. Good and evil were more recognizable there than from the trenches of Flanders or the jungles of Vietnam. But even there—remember Hiroshima?—there was no glory in war to inspire us.

Our psalms come from another time. War was hardly less hideous then, wounding face to face, with no painkillers available. But the psalms remain, packed full of swords and shields, slings and spears, the shattering of cities and the slaying of soldiers. God is the one who trains for battle; God is the one who fights the harshest; God is the one to whom victory is due. We acclaim God of Sabaoth, the leader of a host of angelic armies, destroying the enemy so that one people can live. What can our language do with all these metaphors of war? What is here besides our utter distaste?

One image survives from all this military science: God as stronghold.

> *My eyes are fixed on you, O my Strength;*
> *for you, O God, are my stronghold.*
> *My merciful God comes to meet me;*
> *God will let me look in triumph on my enemies.*
> —*Psalm 59*

Stronghold: God as a fastness for us in fear; God as a keep for our treasure; God as a citadel after the climb; God as a tower situated so high that we can see the safest path; God as a fortress whose walls resist attack. So is God a stronghold: God is not only the weapons of war but the protection from war. In this stronghold, using the arms God provides, we live secure. For the arms God offers are God's own arms, which by enfolding us in godly life make our life the more human. For the stronghold of God is the divine embrace. We are held through the night of tears; we are caught up as we fall into the depths; we delight to be hugged by the bear who is God. "Hold me up, and I shall be safe," says the psalmist, and so Peter is pulled up from the waves by the outstretched arms of Christ.

But finally, there in the psalms, the stronghold becomes a walled garden of peace:

> *The LIVING GOD of power and might is with us;*
> *the God of Jacob is our stronghold.*
> *There is a river whose streams make glad the city of God,*
> *the holy habitation of the Most High.*
> *Come now and look upon the works of the LIVING ONE,*
> *what awesome things God has done on earth.*

It is the LIVING GOD who makes war to cease in all the world,
who breaks the bow, and shatters the spear,
and burns the shields with fire.
The LIVING GOD of power and might is with us;
the God of Jacob is our stronghold.
—Psalm 46

A stronghold is not only an accessory to war and a protection from war, but also the end of war. God is not only victory, but also peace. The image is more than we first believed.

GOD'S GROVE OF TREES:

The first is the tree of life set in Eden, the tree from which we have not yet eaten. But an old legend says that Seth took a seed from that sacred tree and planted it in the grave in Father Adam's mouth. From that seed grew a towering tree from which emanated healing powers; from that tree was built a wooden bridge over the waters at Siloam (and there the Queen of Sheba prophesied a coming glory); and, finally, from that ramshackle bridge's scrap lumber was constructed a cross, which when exhumed by pious Queen Helena restored a dead man to life. From that seed had come the true cross.

Was that tree a gopher tree, used for the lumber of Noah's ark? Was this tree of life a tamarisk tree, which along with Sarah's tomb, was all Abraham owned in the promised land? Was this tree of life a palm tree, shading wise Deborah as she judged God's people Israel? Was the tree a cedar, becoming one of the walls of God's house, the temple in Jerusalem? Or perhaps a cypress, used for the sanctified floor? Was it perhaps the broom tree under which rested Elijah before he walked up to the mountain of God? Was the tree an apple tree, hovering over the lovers, she singing a canticle, his upraised trunk spilling over and filling his love with fruit?

And what kind of tree was Jesse's tree, appearing dried up but marking a stump, now a twig, now a branch, finally a tree of life? Was Jesse's tree the fig tree under which Nathaniel sat when he was found and named by the Messiah? Was Jesse's tree the sycamore, up which half-pint Zacchaeus would climb to catch a glimpse of God?

Perhaps it is the olive tree of God's people, onto which we broken branches are grafted.

Most likely the tree is all these: gopher, tamarisk, palm, cedar, cypress, broom, apple and fig, sycamore and olive, and yet two more. For the tree in the city of God at the end of time grows twelve different fruits, and its leaves can heal the nations: a sacred woodland from a single trunk.

Over my desk hangs a reproduction of Hannah Cohoon's "Tree of Life." Hannah Cohoon, who showed up one day with her two children ("no record was found of her marriage," the museum plaque found it necessary to say) in Hancock, Massachusetts, joined the Shaker community there. She is known to us today by name, as precious few Shakers are, because she painted religious symbols. Hannah's drawings are art: this picture a mighty tree with checkered leaves and fruit round and full, greens and orange and gold, like fecund sunflowers, the leaves and fruits far too large for such a slender trunk but somehow perfectly balanced in a holy air. The Shakers revered the Tree of Life, which they, the elect, would enjoy—not now, but some day.

In illustrating *Pilgrim's Progress*, William Blake drew the Tree of Life sheltering the pilgrim Christian on his journey. It is clearly a tree —roots, trunk, branches, leaves and fruit. But this tree of life illustrates a passage in which the Christian has a vision of the cross. So it has been in Christian symbolism—the tree of God is both in Paradise and on Calvary. In Acts, Peter already says that "He was hanged on a tree," and Simone Weil writes of living "naked and nailed to the Tree of Life."

The tree of our God is the cross; our Yggdrasil—that mythic Norse ash tree binding earth and heaven and hell—is the crucifix. Bonaventure's "Tree of Life" makes the branches of the great tree the truths of the mystery of Christ. Yet the cross becomes one not only with the tree of life but also with the tree of knowledge of good and evil, that tree which in confirming the humanity of Eve and Adam gave them death. Did John, at the foot of the cross, catch sight of the serpent, slithering in the shadows of the taboo crosspiece? For on Passion Sunday we affirm that the one "who by a tree once overcame might by a tree be overcome."

"The trees of nature fruitless be, compared with Christ, the apple tree," says the 1784 hymn. And since the tree is Christ, we become trees:

> *The righteous shall flourish like a palm tree,*
> *and shall spread abroad like a cedar of Lebanon.*
> *Those who are planted in the house of the* LIVING ONE
> *shall flourish in the courts of our God;*
> *They shall still bear fruit in old age;*
> *they shall be green and succulent.*
>
> —*Psalm 92*

But the tree is Christ; so the tree is God, "your shade at your right hand, whose leaves will heal the nations" (Psalm 121).

WOULD THAT MOST artists had left the angels off their canvasses and out of their marble! Armored goddesses, robed young men, flying beasties, feminine beauties, even toddler angels with pink winglets: these silly representations are incised in our brains, and we cannot hear of angels without remembering laughable Christmas cards. Such works of art at the least diminish our imagination and, at worst, render the word "angels" powerless in our religious language.

In the ancient stories, one is never sure whether it is God or an angel who is present. The angel, a representation of the divine, a bearer of God's grace, is a manner of Godself being among us. Samson's parents exclaim their terror at meeting an angel by saying, "We have seen God." Angels are ways of God's being seen, a step toward God's presence, the ears, mouth and hands of God.

There are (some say) four archangels: Michael, slayer of the dragon; Gabriel, guardian of Paradise; Raphael, healer and guide; and finally, Uriel. Of Uriel—meaning God's fire—little is known, and the name itself is found only in apocryphal Jewish writings that never made their way onto Christian bookshelves. U is for Uriel, the non-canonical archangel, one of the four who hold up the throne of God. They say it is Uriel who polices Eden's tree of life, who wrestled with Jacob, who killed Egypt's firstborn, who slew Sennacherib's army, who blockades Hades. Some say it was God who warned Noah of the coming flood, but others say God sent Uriel on this deathly task. Uriel is the dark arm of God, the dread news, the discipline and the struggle. Vengeance is mine, says the LIVING GOD. Uriel is the divine hand that holds the line on kindness, the divine eyes that foresee destruction, and the holy mouth that speaks punishment.

We appliquè cute flames onto Pentecost banners—but the consuming fire which is godly Uriel is hardly some blessed can of Sterno keeping our holy fondue bubbly. Remember Sodom and Gomorrah, where the smoke of the land went up like smoke from a furnace? Fiery Uriel is burning up God's enemies on every side, melting the wicked as if they were made of wax. The psalms even give us words to pray for Uriel's fire:

Fight those who fight me, O LIVING ONE;
  attack those who are attacking me.
Let them be like chaff before the wind,
  and let the angel of the LIVING GOD
  drive them away.

                                          —Psalm 35

For while it is dangerous to say, "See here, see there," and equate the disasters around us with God's avenging fire, we'd best not imagine that God's flames have gone completely out. Indeed, the burning martyrs said that on Good Friday as well as on Pentecost the fire of God was blazing. Uriel must have been the angel who came to minister on Calvary.

Before we can pray for fire on others we must be ready to expect some burns ourselves. Despite the more simpleminded psalms, God's flames sear also the faithful:

How long will you be angry, O LIVING ONE?
Will your fury blaze like fire forever?

For the stories do say that Uriel is there, a fire of consuming rage, one of the four messengers of God.

ONCE THERE WAS a magnificent mountain, a sight fit for mooning poets or the lone adventurer: meadow grasses and wild flowers, pines and streams, the mirror lake, and—displacing the clouds, perhaps holding up the sky itself—the green, purple and finally white shape of the classic mountain summit. Photographers would await a clear day, and faraway folks enjoyed the postcard, delighting to know that in this world of chaos and ugliness was this living rainbow of natural balance, natural perfection.

The name of this mountain is Mount St. Helens, and photographers passing by on May 18, 1980, caught the other half of all this stunning beauty. All was over; for decades the place will be desolate. The volcano's peak was blown off, and every tree and flower incinerated by the devastating heat. The lake has actually disappeared. All color was enwrapped in a gray shroud, and even 3000 miles away the New York sky was soured by the mountain's belch. We who claim to understand the volcanic process stood quietly, filtering our breath, stunned by this image of destruction. And although we logged its dozen subsequent eruptions, measured the grit, calculated the flaming rocks and analyzed the steam, we, for at least some moments, experienced a primal terror, for this volcano is greater than we are.

Insurance companies seldom grant protection against volcanic damage. The total destruction is termed "an act of God," a catastrophe outpacing precaution, devastation beyond reckoning. Beyond. Beyond. If the spectacle of the mountain's glory is beyond our description, yet more so is the horror of the ash. The scriptures describe God as the One beyond: beyond what we understand, beyond what we have, beyond what we are. El Shaddai was Abraham's name for God: the God of the mountain peak, the God as unfathomable as that distant glory, as enigmatic as a mount with its power and its beauty. The tradition has translated El Shaddai only as "Almighty God"; the image has been lost. The mountain, which now we scale with climbing equipment and measure with laboratory instruments, has been replaced by the ambiguous adjective "almighty," so thoughtlessly spoken that a child might think that "almighty" is God's first name.

Almighty: a vague modifier, especially inadequate to answer the question itself it suggests: Why does God, that God of all might, permit evil in the world? God of the mountain peaks, rather, offers a specific image, a picture of mystery, dearness but otherness, the beloved yet unknown summit of the land.

The image of God of the mountain is not, fortunately, only an idyll, a crag for Wordsworth to contemplate while strolling in the meadow. The God beyond is also the end of the mountain, the volcano itself.

The earth reeled and rocked;
   the roots of the mountains shook;
   they reeled because of God's anger.
Smoke arose from God's nostrils
and a consuming fire from the mouth of the LIVING ONE,
   with hot burning coals blazing forth.
The LIVING ONE was enwrapped in darkness,

> *cloaked in dark waters and thick clouds.*
> *From the brightness of God's presence, through the clouds,*
>   *burst hailstones and coals of fire.*
> *The LIVING ONE thundered out of heaven;*
> *the voice of the Most High spoke out.*
> —*Psalm 18*

God-as-mountain talk is mush unless it is mixed with God-as-volcano, just as theology of reconciliation is foolishness unless first there is terror before the God beyond.

God is still beyond: the volcano laying waste our daisies, destroying our idylls. No small task, this, to find images in the modern consciousness for power beyond. Perhaps we could talk of space: not our local space littered with used-up spaceships, but the space beyond the space beyond, the going-out-forever past the solar systems, the never-endingness, the no-edge to the universe, the space from which we have not yet seen light. Not God as the cloud's silver lining, but God as black hole, the star mass with gravity so great that not only can its light not escape, but its darkness in the end will engulf the universe. Not God as the rays of the sun, but God as the center of the sun.

THE SCRIBES WROTE, "In the beginning God created.
. . ." At first it was enough to give God's title, just "God," the God who
is God, and to declare that God created the world. But language
moves toward specificity: What we believe to be significant we dis-
tinguish linguistically from neighbors near and far. So the simple
noun God was soon found to be insufficient.

So to the question "But how did God create the world?" the
ancient Hebrews sang a clarification:

> *God who by wisdom made the heavens,*
> *whose mercy endures for ever.*
>
> *—Psalm 136*

What is it about God that created the world? Wisdom. What did God
use to create the world? Divine wisdom alone. Now we have a handle
on this untouchable God: Wisdom. For we know about wisdom, the

workings of mind meshed with compassion. We can understand a little bit of God: Wisdom.

So much did divine wisdom occupy imaginations that a figure was born, a mighty woman springing fully armed from the poet's head: Lady Wisdom herself, whom God created first in the primeval time of creating. Lady Wisdom was God's companion, God's help, for creating the universe. The Hebrew writers prized her judgment, her stature, her beauty. This first-begotten of God stands by life's pathways and points us to her home in God. Later, Jews speaking Greek called her Sophia, the Wise Woman, a feminine personification of essential wisdom in the omniscient God. In some poems she reigns so triumphantly that she is presented as the divine consort, the very woman of God.

But imaginations ran also in a second direction. To that question, "With what did God create the world?" came a second answer:

By the word of the LIVING ONE were the heavens made.
—*Psalm 33*

God spoke in Genesis: Let there be, and there was. Not God's sight, no divine agent, but the spoken word creates. So there developed also a tradition about the powerful word calling into being that which it names, the divine word creating reality by bringing order out of chaos. The Hebrew scriptures attest that God's word saves, condemns, blesses, destroys. It is God's word which the prophets speak, a burning coal on the lips, a sweet scroll to swallow.

In the Book of Wisdom, Jews writing in Greek wed these two together. Sophia and Logos, wisdom and word, are interchangeably invoked as the names of God. God's wisdom, God's word—that is what we praise. The God who is wisdom and word is the God who knows us and by whom we are named. The way was set, the vocabulary prepared, the metaphors merged, so that two centuries later John's prologue could be written. In the beginning—the same story told again, anew—was the Word: God's speech was made into Jesus. All things were made through him: Sophia becomes Christ.

Wisdom, Word: potholders for the sacred tripod. Wisdom, Word: God is personified by human attributes which are our pride—we like God, having wisdom, speaking words. Yet Paul writes that the wisdom of God is the opposite of ours: folly, foolishness, absurdity. And Mark suggests that the Word spoke most powerfully when he endured his passion in silence.

X IS FOR xat. A xat is a totem pole, a sacred pillar that designates the center of the earth by connecting the next world with this one. On the xat are images of the dead ancestors, their faces becoming a holy line between the people and their deities, marking the journey to God. Here, claims the xat, the dead went up. Here the gods and goddesses came down. The dead, affixed in the air, are part-way up, and the living honor their progress.

Tradition says that St. Andrew was martyred on an X-shaped cross. The Gospel of John names Andrew as the first disciple to follow Jesus, and a life of faithfulness ended by his mounting his xat, hanging there midway to God. The church commemorates Andrew near the beginning of Advent. It is as if as each year commences we approach a Christian xat, Andrew leading us up through death to God.

There's one more X. Do merchants who choose the safe word Xmas realize that the X is the first letter of the Greek spelling of Christ? It is not that X substitutes the secular for the religious, an unknown mathematical quantity taking the place of the baby born. Rather, the

X is Christ, who was himself lifted on a sacred pole, the ancestor going to God before us, the one whose faithfulness trained Andrew for the journey.

And not only Andrew. We all know very little of the next world, the faraway realm of the divine. We do know, however, about Andrew's X and Christ's X. To understand this xat, Christians heard in the ancient psalm the voice of Christ:

> *Draw near to me and redeem me;*
> *because of my enemies deliver me.*
> *They gave me gall to eat,*
> *and when I was thirsty, they gave me vinegar to drink.*
> *As for me, I am afflicted and in pain;*
> *your help, O God, will lift me high.*
>
> *—Psalm 69*

As the Gospel of John testified, when Christ was lifted up on that high cross, he drew the whole world to himself. With Andrew and the dying Jesus, we commend ourselves to God, going up through our death toward divine life. We attend the xat of Christ, and honor its holy ground, this X our way to God, this X in some mysterious way a letter in God's name.

OUR YOKE IS our god. Whatever it is that we walk by, whoever it is that guides us, that is our god. The pattern we choose to follow, the frame we fit ourselves into, that is our god. We are not so liberated as we like to believe; most of us willingly don a yoke. It helps us walk the furrows without wandering aimlessly. It helps us plow our fields.

Best, then, if our God is our yoke. God's yoke, we say, is the easy wood, shaped differently from any regular ox-yoke, worn so thoroughly already by another that the wood is worn light. The saints who delighted to wear the yoke walked in the strangest directions, as if this yoke is one which takes old furrows away.

Think of Clare of Assisi, running away from home, refusing middle-class marriage and motherhood, embracing poverty and prayer. Think of Harriet Tubman, walking back down south yet again, searching for some slaves to sneak up to freedom.

But furrows or not, a yoke binds together two burdened beasts. We share the toil, we breathe in concert and pull together. In binding us to one another, the yoke consoles. In joining us to Christ, the yoke saves. Indeed, with God as the yoke, we are coupled one to another by the very self of God.

> *Happy are they whose way is blameless,*
>   *who walk in the law of the LIVING ONE!*
> *When your word goes forth it gives light;*
>   *it gives understanding to the simple.*
> *I open my mouth and pant;*
>   *I long for your commandments.*
> *Turn to me in mercy,*
>   *as you always do to those who love your name.*
>   *—Psalm 119*

ENOUGH METAPHORS, WE say. We want God
face to face. But all we get this side of death is yet another metaphor.
So we conclude our metaphors as does the Bible: by entering the city
of Zion.

> Beautiful and lofty, the joy of all the earth, is the hill of Zion,
> the city of the great Sovereign and the very center of the world.
> Make a circuit of Zion;
> Walk round about it;
>   count the number of its towers.
> Consider well its bulwarks;
> examine its strongholds,
>   that you may tell those who come after:
> "This God is our God for ever and ever."
>
> —Psalm 48

Heading toward the city, up the mountain they rise, Anna and Andrew, Miriam and Monica. Blinded and burned by Uriel's fire, up they mount, up the mountain of Zion. Bathed in the river, nursed by the cup, surrounded by saints, blown to bits in the volcano, sailing through the dark of noon, up to their Sovereign the Queen. Come up, come here, for this is the night the law begins dancing. Come, shepherd, and exult in the stronghold hidden in the skeletal tree. What is that? A rock? A phoenix? A gemstone? Arise, ascend, you ill, you hungry, you burdened, you enslaved. You need no wisdom, you need no words; the song soars before you. Up we leap; God will lead. Up, up the mountain of Zion, we rise to gaze at God.

> *Of the city it shall be said, "Everyone was born in Zion."*
> *The singers and the dancers will say,*
> *"All my fresh springs are in you."*
> *—Psalm 87*

But as we think we see Zion in the clouds, we discover the city has already come down from the sky. It is here all around us. The mountain has become a plain. We had thought to search around Zion, its throne room, its banquet halls and gardens, but here is God's Zion, everywhere about, before us, behind. The dance is now. The springs are here. Zion has come to us.

Anna . . . Bath . . .
Cup . . . David . . .
According to one
legend, the first
thing that God
created was the
Hebrew alphabet,
from which God
proceeded to form
everything else.
Queen . . . Rock . . .
Stronghold . . . In
this book we walk
through our own
alphabet to see, if
not everything, at
least 26 things that
are in God and of
God. Wisdom . . .
Yoke . . . Zion.

Liturgy Training
Publications
ISBN 1-56854-071-X
$8.00
P/MGOD

PMGOD

9781568540719

A Metaphorical God

An Abecedary of Images for God

by

Gail Ramshaw

Art by Rita Corbin

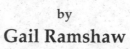